GOOGLE CLASSROOM

The Complete Guide for Teachers to Create and Manage a Virtual Classroom

BY
GERALD TODD

© Copyright 2020 by Gerald Todd
All rights reserved.

This document is geared towards providing exact and reliable information with regards to the topic and issue covered. The publication is sold with the idea that the publisher is not required to render accounting, officially permitted, or otherwise, qualified services. If advice is necessary, legal or professional, a practiced individual in the profession should be ordered.

- From a Declaration of Principles which was accepted and approved equally by a Committee of the American Bar Association and a Committee of Publishers and Associations.

In no way is it legal to reproduce, duplicate, or transmit any part of this document in either electronic means or in printed format. Recording of this publication is strictly prohibited and any storage of this document is not allowed unless with written permission from the publisher. All rights reserved.

The information provided herein is stated to be truthful and consistent, in that any liability, in terms of inattention or otherwise, by any usage or abuse of any policies, processes, or directions contained within is the solitary and utter responsibility of the recipient reader. Under no circumstances will any legal responsibility or blame be held against the publisher for any reparation, damages, or monetary loss due to the information herein, either directly or indirectly.

Respective authors own all copyrights not held by the publisher.

The information herein is offered for informational purposes solely, and is universal as so. The presentation of the information is without contract or any type of guarantee assurance.

The trademarks that are used are without any consent, and the publication of the trademark is without permission or backing by the trademark owner. All trademarks and brands within this book are for clarifying purposes only and are the owned by the owners themselves, not affiliated with this document.

CONTENTS

Introduction --- 4

Chapter 1: Google Classroom -- 6

Chapter 2: Google Classroom As A Tool For Active Learning ------ 10

Chapter 3: How To Set Up Google Classroom ------------------------ 43

Chapter 4: Tips To Get The Most Out Of Google Classroom ------- 47

Chapter 5: Google Classroom Can Help With Home-Schooling----- 58

Chapter 6: Lockdown Drives Immense Demand For Google Classroom App--- 62

Chapter 7: Effectiveness Of Google Classroom ----------------------- 68

Chapter 8: Benefits And Limitations Of Google Classroom -------- 71

Chapter 9: Awesome Apps That Incorporate With Google Classroom--- 76

Chapter 10: Frequently Asked Questions ------------------------------ 91

Conclusion --- 100

INTRODUCTION

Google Classroom is a free web-based platform that allows you to manage your resources, assignments, planning, and contact with your students. If your school doesn't already have one, you'll need to sign up for Google Apps for Education account to use Google Classroom to provide you with all the features of Google Apps including Docs, Sheets, Drive, Gmail, and Calendar. Available on laptops, phones, and desktops, Google Classroom is accessible for both teachers and students.

Google Classroom helps organize your Digital Classroom. It sits on top of Google Drive and builds files to keep yourself and your students organized for each class and each assignment. You and the students can attach files from your Google Drive to the Classroom, and all files transferred via Google Classroom are automatically stored in Google Drive.

Teachers and students can keep track of all due assignments, and teachers can see who has completed their work and respond to the students in real-time. Work may also be assessed and resubmitted, if necessary.

Google Classroom is a great way to introduce students to methods for communicating/collaborating and accessing information online in a safe and easily accessible, self-contained environment. Google Classroom can be implemented in elementary school and used fully in middle and high school. Recent research (Getting the Most from Google Classroom) shows that while working on assignments, Google Classroom greatly increases the students' accessibility to materials and collaboration.

More than likely, you already have a Google account, and G Suite for Education has been registered with your school district technology administrator. Unless the district has not yet enrolled, the organization must be licensed by a school administrator and the staff and students must create Google accounts. That person will also need to make sure that Google Classroom is turned on and adds you as a teacher to create courses.

The amazing thing about Google Classroom is that it's self-contained so that only people in your domain have access to it, and it provides a level of privacy for school-age children. On the other hand, because of the privacy rules, you'll find that you cannot share your classroom with others outside your school domain. Guardians, if this option is turned on, will provide email summaries of their student development.

Chapter 1:

GOOGLE CLASSROOM

The Google Classroom is an ongoing development of Google for academic organizations to guarantee a blended learning platform to simplify creating, distributing, and grading assignments in a paperless way. It combines online multimedia with conventional classroom techniques. It is a helpful way for the teachers to draw in students online for asking questions, looking at any topic with the teacher and classmates, and submitting assignments.

As S. Iftakhar states, "Google classroom permits teachers to invest more time with their students and less time on administrative work, and that is much better. Google's most recent edition brings new functionality to Google Classroom. The new Google Classroom functionality can include more than one teacher, to prepare for classes."

How it functions

Google Classroom is not a well-known platform for many of us. So, a guideline to set up Google Classroom is given here for clear understanding:

A. Visit classroom.google.com. The earlier version of Google Classroom was associated with organization based email addresses. Therefore, just teachers and students having an institute based domain could use Google Classroom. In March 2017, Google opened the classroom to permit personal Google users to join classes without the necessity of having a G Suite for Education account. In April, it became possible for any personal Google user to create and teach a class.

B. Click on the "+" button to create your first class. You can see the "+" button close to your email address. Press on the "Create Class" button.

C. Include a class name and a section, for instance, Listening Skill; Section: A

D. You can include details of your class in the "About" tab. You can include a class description and guidelines for the students. You can similarly refer to which room students meet for their traditional classes. The teacher's email address and Google Drive organizer for classroom materials can also be included. You can add your course layout and lesson plan at the bottom.

E. Now students can join the classroom. If they have an

institutional Google account, it is simpler to join. Request that they sign in to Google Classroom through their accounts. They need to click the "+" button, and it will request a class code.
F. Find your class code in the "Stream" tab and tell your students the code they will need to join your classroom.

If students don't have the institutional Google account, request that they create an individual Google account. Collect their Google accounts and welcome them to join Google Classroom in the "Students" tab. In this instance, students won't require any class code to join your classroom.

FEATURES OF GOOGLE CLASSROOM

- When the classroom is ready to work, you will discover a "+" button at the bottom right of the screen. You can do the following exercises in Google Classroom by clicking on it:
- Create announcements: This section is used for reporting any sort of update about the class. You can transfer documents, Google Drive, recordings, and web links as class materials too.
- Create assignments: This is the most significant component of Google Classroom. Here you can post an assignment which students are to submit by a deadline. As in the announcement section, you can transfer documents, Google Drive,

recordings, and web links. Students can see their assignment in the class "Stream". They can download materials and complete their assignments. On the top right, they will see three options (Turn-In, Comments, and Share). They should select "Turn In". A window will request that they confirm. They need to click on the blue box marked "Turn In" to confirm their submission. As a teacher, you will get an email notification of the submission of the assignment. You will have the option to check all the assignments and grade them. At long last, you can assess the assignments give your feedback, and give grades.

- Create question: This area is used to ask a question and discuss answers with students. Here students can edit their answers and reply to one another if the teacher permits.
- Reuse post: In this section teachers can reuse any significant post (announcement, assignment, or a question) that they had used before in this classroom or another classroom.

Chapter 2:

Google Classroom as a Tool for Active Learning

As new technologies are being developed, finding and controlling new concepts and ideas of online education are evolving quickly. Because of these changes, many states, organizations, and institutions have been working on new methods to improve online education. This book assesses the effectiveness of Google Classroom's dynamic learning activities under the Decision Sciences program. Technology Acceptance Model (TAM) has been used to measure the viability of the learning exercises. An aggregate of 100 responses from students who selected data extraction was used in this study. The outcomes showed that a larger part of the students were satisfied with the Google Classroom's device that was presented in the class. The result of the data analyzed demonstrated that all ratios are above midpoints. Specifically, performance is acceptable in the area of simple access, perceived helpfulness, communication and association, guidance delivery, and student fulfillment concerning the Google Classroom's dynamic learning exercises.

Google is a well-known Web 2.0 tool that offers a lot of interesting facilities and apps. It, in the same way as other Web 2.0 tools, has the potential for educating and learning given its exceptional built-in capacities that offer instructive, social, and technological advantages.

Google Classroom is another tool presented in Google Apps for Education in 2014. This classroom encourages the teachers to make and sort out assignments quickly, give feedback efficiently, and speak to their classes with ease.

The current traditional strategy for educating is teacher-focused learning where lecturers use visual guides such as presentation slides, whiteboard interactive screens. Learning exercises in the P.C. lab is one of the difficulties in higher education. A subject that is a practical exercise, for example, Data Extraction is commonly illustrative or demonstrated in the P.C. lab that stresses the acquisition of observational skills; and permit students to see the idea managed in action and relate the hypothesis more closely to reality. It is essential to consider objectives, aims, and objectives in the context of laboratory work. However, the students' response to practical work is often negative as a result they are not successful in lab work, and this may reflect a student's perception that there is a lack of a clear reason for the hands-on lab task. P.C. lab educating in colleges is often criticized for being prescribed, impersonal, lacking an open door for individual judgments and creativity due to the lack of time, for instance, data extraction class in undergrad level is given just three hours out of every week.

The effectiveness of Google classroom's dynamic learning exercises for data extraction class.

The remainder of the book is organized as follows: in the following segment, a survey of related works is given, followed by the research method used in this study. The outcomes and discoveries are then clarified and condensed.

RELATED WORKS

Online education keeps on developing and is playing a huge role in Malaysian higher education.

- Shea and Bidjerano said in its rapid development, research is beginning to prove, that online education has risen above the "no significant difference". For over ten years, the acknowledged wisdom has been that online education and its forerunner, "distance learning" brought about no significant difference comparative with learning outcomes accomplished through classroom instruction.

TAM was developed by

- Davis to clarify the computer-usage conduct. There are two significant determinants of the actual framework used:

perceived ease of use (PEOU) and perceived usefulness (P.U.).
- Saadé, Nebebe, and Tan required that college students' participation and involvement were important to an essential e-learning framework, and therefore, students' acknowledgment should be evaluated. They suggested that TAM was a solid theoretical model where its validity can extend to the e-learning context.

In the context of integration of Google classroom into the teaching and learning of data extraction and related apps, the users (teachers or students) must understand that Google classroom is valuable in aiding in the teaching and learning process. The teacher's responsibilities are to make students aware of its use in the future work environment, just as to show students that it is not difficult to use.

Google Classroom can be used as an educational/psychological tool to help in changing the focal point of the classroom from one that is teacher-focused and controlled to one that is learner-focused and open to questions, dialogue, and creative awareness involving students as dynamic members. The use of Google classroom in educating and learning data extraction and related apps is proposed to be used as a psychological/instructive tool. Using Google classroom additionally improves higher-order thinking skills, advances the improvement of problem-solving skills, and supports "imagine a scenario where…"

type questions which are needed in this P.C. age.

According to the online form, the social mix is identified with feelings of group understanding.

- Academic integration, student fulfillment in intellectual development, is less reliant on the type of communication when compared with social integration.

From the literature review, it was discovered that Google classroom is required in the future work environment of business graduates.

The Teacher's Guide to Google Classroom

Google Classroom is a free app intended to support students and teachers communicate, team up, organize and oversee assignments, go paperless, and substantially more!

This guide is filled with step by step guidelines for using Google Classroom, setting up classes, making announcements, conversations, assignments, assignment management, and tips! You will also discover helpful screen captures of both the teacher and student side of Google Classroom. This reference guide is great for new users and loaded with convenient updates and tips for more experienced users.

Things You Should Know:

- GAFE: Google Classroom is accessible to the user with Google Apps for Education (GAFE), a free shared suite of tools that incorporates web tools like Google Docs, Gmail, Google Drive, and more. If you have a GAFE account and don't have access to Google Classroom, contact your school or area I.T. division.
- Grade levels: Google Classroom can be used at any grade level, contingent upon the skill of the teacher and the abilities of the students. Students should have the option to log in to Google Classroom using their Google Apps credentials. Most teachers are discovering success in fourth grade, and up, however, there are many using it in primary as well.
- Google Chrome: To make the best use of the features in Google Classroom, teachers and students should use the Google Chrome Browser. A few features work in a different browser, however not all. Also, Google Chrome is a great learning source for everything Google!
- Menus: Google uses two images across Google Classroom, and other Google apps (including mobile apps) to open menus and more activities:

Three lines = menu (normally the main menu)

Three dots= more actions (additional options and activities)

Whenever you see these symbols, there are extra features, actions, or options to explore.

Google Classroom

Google Classroom is intended to support teachers and students to communicate and team up, oversee assignments paperlessly, and remain organized. Google Classroom is a part of the Google Apps for Education suite of tools and is only accessible to Google Apps for Education accounts.

First Login

Go to classroom.google.com.. Look down and pick your role: teacher or student.

- Teacher role: Can create and join classes in Google Classroom.
- Student role: Can ONLY join classes in Google Classroom.

Note: You can't change your role later, so make certain to choose the right one. If you or your students select the wrong role, you should contact your Google Apps I.T. executive to address the error.

Make or Join a Class

Click on the + at the top option to take a class, or get a class together with the class code.

CREATE AND CUSTOMIZE YOUR CLASS

1. **Create and Name Your Class**

Click on the + to create a class. Use a logical naming system for your class name, and be consistent over all of your classes.

Beginners Tip: Create your classes in reverse order. For instance, if you teach seven class periods, make the seventh-period class first, then sixth, then fifth, etc. This will permit you to see your classes on the Google Classroom home page in sequential order, which you will see later in this guide.

2. **Take the Tour (It's advisable!)**

There is an important tour incorporated with Google Classroom for both the students and teachers. It is worth your time to take a couple of minutes to get to know the app.

3. **Upload Photo or Select Theme**

Upload your image or select a theme from the gallery (Note: The picture must be at least 800x200 pixels.)

Include Class Details

The "About tab" is the place you include the details of your class, which includes syllabus, materials, course description, invite co-teachers and more.

ADD CLASS MATERIALS

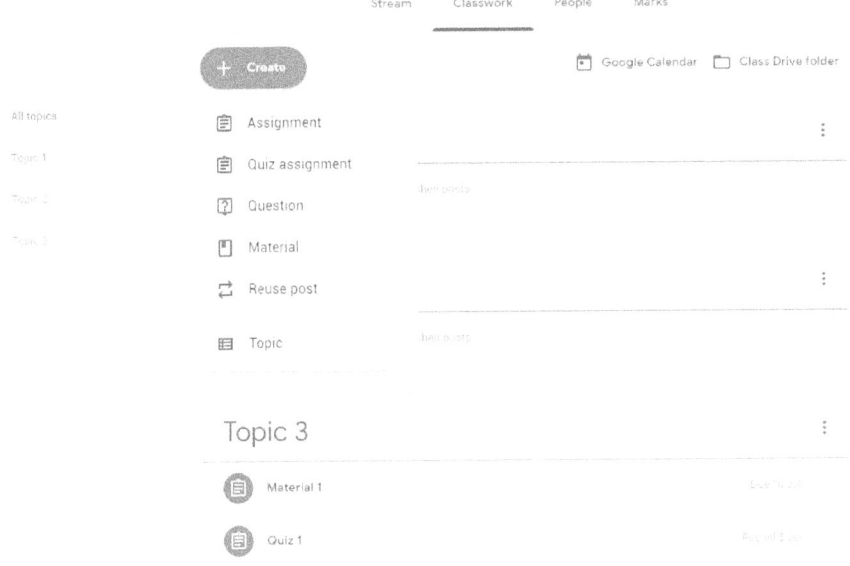

The About tab is additionally a great hub for your classroom resources. Consider including files like:

- Class Syllabus,
- Google Slide,
- Class Rules,
- Google Drive or Google Doc
- and other files that students will need all through the school year.

Include the heading of your materials and append your resources and files from Google Drive, local storage, YouTube videos. Click on "POST" to save.

ADDING STUDENTS

Add Students using the Class Code: When you make a class, the Classroom will produce a class code that you can provide for your students that will permit them to join your lesson. This six-digit code is unique to your space and your class. The class code can be found in the left sidebar of the stream, and the Students tab.

If necessary, you can reset this code or stop access to it once all your students have joined.

How Students Join with the Class Code:

Give this code to your students. Students will follow the method below.

1. Go to classroom.google.com. If it is their first login, make certain to guide them to choose their role as students.
2. Click on the + on the upper right of the page to Join a class.
3. Enter the Class Code and click on Join.

The most effective method to Invite Students:

This strategy requires more work on the part of the teacher. So more often than not, I suggest using the class code strategy. Follow the method below to invite your students separately.

1. To invite students, they should be in your Google contacts. Your Google App administrator may have made student contacts or groups for you. If not, you should add all of your students to your contacts. To do this, go to google.com/contacts, and make a new contact for every student OR make a contact group for every one of your classes.
2. After setting up your class, go to the Students tab and click on the Invite button.
3. Search for a group or every student and check the box to choose.
4. Click Invite Students.

INVITE CO-TEACHERS

On this page, you will be able to invite a co-teacher on the left-hand side. Click on the INVITE TEACHER button to invite a co-teacher to your class. Co-Teachers have the same permissions as teachers in the class.

Here you can alternatively add extra class details and link to other data.

1. The title of your class
2. Room number
3. Class description
4. Click to see the Class folder that has been created on Google

Drive.

5. Click to view your class schedule in a new tab.
6. Click SAVE to save your changes.

THE STREAM

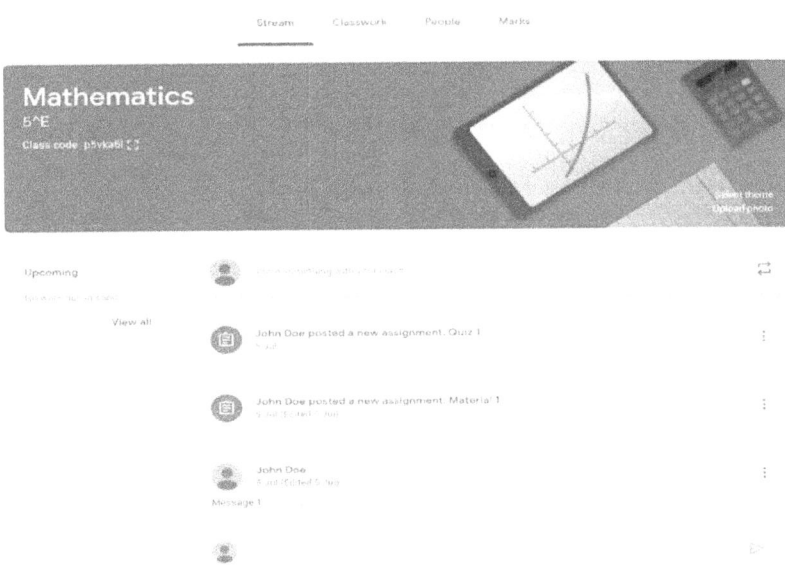

This is where educators view and add declarations, assignments, comments, and discussion topics.

Add content to the Stream: Use the "plus" in the bottom right of the screen to create:

1. Announcements: This is an exceptional method to speak with

your students, share reminders, updates, and school announcements or general classes.
2. Assignments: Create computerized assignments with due dates and make a paperless work process for students and teachers.
3. Questions for Discussion: Pose a short answer question for your students to talk about.
4. Reuse Posts: Reuse any past announcement, question, or assignment again in any class.

Alternatively, add other material to your posts:

1. File Attachments: records saved locally on your device or computer.
2. Google Drive: Files saved in your Google Drive.
3. YouTube recordings
4. Web Links to third party websites, resources, etc.

COMMENT SETTINGS

In the Students Tab, you will discover a dropdown menu to set your preferences for student remarks in Google Classroom.

You have three choices:

1. Students can comment and post: (This is the default setting.)

This means students can make their posts and add to the stream. Comments and remarks are an effective way to support correspondence and cooperation in the classroom. Set a few rules and monitor constantly.
2. Students can ONLY comment: This means students can drop their comments on the instructor's posts in the stream. This is an appropriate method to permit questions, explanations, and keep communicating with students.
3. ONLY the instructor/teachers can comment or post: Any students inside Google Classroom cannot add comments.

Note: The teacher/educator can generally observe ALL of the comments, even after they have been deleted. In the stream, there is a flip button to "show erased things." Flip the switch and see what's been deleted. Ensure your students understand that everything they post is under your supervision!

STUDENT'S VIEW: THE STREAM

The stream is where students can access and view assignments, discussion topics, announcements, and comments. Whenever enabled by the teacher, students can also leave comments and add posts. (See the Communication section for additional details on these settings.)

The following are reminders and directions for students.

Add a Student Post to the Stream:

Click on the + in the bottom right of the screen, and afterward pick Create a post.

- Add the content of your class post. Keep in mind; this is viewable by your teacher and the whole class.
- Use the post to pose an inquiry about assignments or class, work with other students in your class, or to share significant resources identified with the topics and class subject.

Note: Your remarks/comments are saved after they have been deleted. Your teacher can generally observe what you share, so keep it appropriate!

Alternatively, add other content to your posts:

- File Attachments: records saved locally on your device or computer.
- Google Drive: Files saved in your Google Drive.
- YouTube recordings
- Web Links to third party websites, resources, etc.

QUESTIONS AND ANNOUNCEMENTS

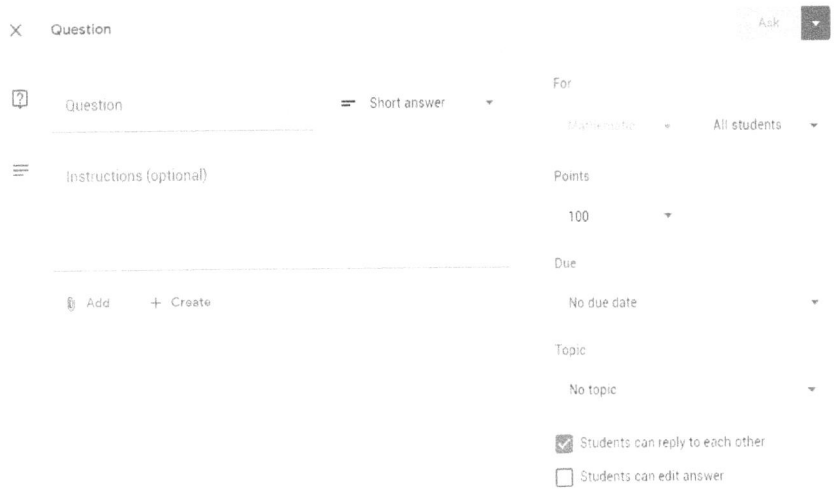

Create Announcements and Questions

1. Click on the "plus" sign in the bottom right corner of the screen.
2. Click on create an announcement.
3. Include the text of your announcement.
4. Select the classes you wish to see the announcement.
5. Alternatively include files, attachments, or links.
6. Click on POST to add to the stream, or save as a draft to post later.

Create a Discussion Question:

1. Click the + in the bottom right corner, and then, click create a

question.
2. Include the content of your question and a description if you like.
3. Input a due date.
4. Select the classes you which to pose the question.
5. Alternatively include files, attachments, or links.
6. Click on ASK to add to the stream, or save it as a draft to post later.
7. After clicking ASK, there will be a pop-up with the accompanying choices to "Let students... "
    a. See and answer to one another's answers
    b. Alter their answers

Select your choices and click ASK.

Student's View: Questions and Announcements

Student's View of Announcements: Announcements will show up in the stream and are read-only; however, students can leave a class comment if the teacher has allowed this. Class comments are readable by the teacher and all students in the class. If the announcement has attachments, the students can also see the documents, videos, or links.

Student's View of Questions in the Stream:

When a conversation question has been given to students, it will promptly show up in the stream. Students will see the accompanying alternatives in the stream.

- Completion Status (done or not done)
- Due Date (Students will also see whether their assignment is Late.)
- Description and Title of the Discussion
- Your Answer: This is where the students input their answers. Students should check their answers before they can view other student's reactions.
- Add a Class Comment: Use this to ask questions or for general remarks. This isn't where you type your response to the inquiry.

Note: The title of the inquiry is clickable and will take students to another page for that question. Students will, in any case, have the choice to type their reaction on this page. However, they will also have the choice to leave a private remark, which is visible by the teacher. Be sure that students know to type their answers in the appropriate answer reaction field, not as a comment or private comment.

ASSIGNMENTS

Create Assignments

1. Click the + in the bottom right corner.
2. Click on the create assignment.
3. Include the title of your task and a discretionary description. (Tip: number your assignments!).
4. Give a due date.
5. Select the classes you are giving the task to.
6. Include files, attachments, or links.
7. Click on ASSIGN to add to the stream, or save it as a draft to post later.

Options:

Assignments with Google Drive records:

When you include Google Slides, Google Sheets, Google Docs, or Google Drawings records as a component of an assignment, you will get extra options for that assignment.

Options:

1. Students can see the document: every student is offered access to a read/view-only form of the record/file.
2. Students can alter documents: every student is offered access to alter and team up on the SAME record/file.
3. Duplicate for every student: every student is given an individual, editable duplicate of the record inside their Google Drive.

STUDENT'S VIEW: ASSIGNMENTS

Student View of Assignments:

Posted assignments will show up in the stream. You might be invited to refresh the assignment or stream to see the most recent updates. Students also have the choice to leave a class remark if the teacher has enabled this. Class remarks are visible by the teacher and all students in the class.

Students will see the accompanying options and information for every assignment in the stream. (Note: This model was made using a Google Doc format and creating a duplicate for every student.)

- Due Date (Students will see if their assignment is Late or not.)
- Completion Status (done or not done)
- Description and Title of the Assignment
- Open: Click on the open button to open the assignment details page.
- Add a Class Comment: Use this space to make questions or for general remarks/comments.

STUDENT'S VIEW: ASSIGNMENT DETAILS

Student View of Assignment Details Page:

Students should build up the ability to click "Open" or tapping on the title of the assignment to open the assignment details page. On this page, students will have extra options for the assignments:

- Description of Assignment, Title, and Due Date.
- Under Your Assignment, Students can view any templates or file attachments the teacher has made or attached for students.

Note: If the teacher has made a layout for students to use, students ought NOT to Add or Create their own except if that is what that the teacher has instructed.

- Add: Here, students can include their documents or links.
- Create: Here, students can make new Slides, Docs, Drawing, or Sheets.
- Turn In: Students click the turn in the button when they have finished the assignment and are prepared to hand it over. Also, they can include a private comment, which is only visible by the teacher.

Student's View: Turn In Assignments

The Turn In Button:

If the teacher has sent a student their duplicate of a Google document type (Slides, Docs, Drawing, or Sheets) as a major part of the assignment, there will also be a Turn In button (upper right) in the Google record by the share button. (Note: The Turn In button changes the responsibility for the record from the student back to the teacher, and the student can no longer alter the document.

Turning In Google Assignments:

Students ought to present their work using the turn in button, NOT by sharing with the teacher. The teacher already has the option to see and alter the file.

Turning In Google Assignments:

At the point when a student taps the turn in button, a pop-up will prompt them to confirm their submission.

Turning In Other Types of Assignments:

If the teacher has chosen a collaborative Google record (student can alter the document), or another external kind of assignment, the student will see a Mark as Done button rather than Turn In. This option will just show up in Google Classroom, not in the record itself.

At the point when students have finished the assignment, they just click on the Mark as Done button to tell the teacher they have finished the assignment. Note: The teacher doesn't get an email notification or alert at the point when work has been turned in or clicked as done. If a student is submitting late work, it is advised that they leave a private comment to inform the teacher of the reasons for the work being late.

STUDENT'S VIEW: UNSUBMIT ASSIGNMENTS

Unsubmit an Assignment:

If the task is a Google archive type, it will be readable just for the student once it has been submitted.

If a student needs to revise or include file attachments, they can click on the Unsubmit button. The document would then be able to be altered and revised once more.

A pop-up update will tell students they should resubmit once they have finished their amendments to the assignment. Click on the Unsubmit button to confirm.

After the student has made their modifications or changed file attachments, they will, at that point, need to click turn in again to resubmit the assignment to Google Classroom.

Managing Assignments: The Stream

Managing Assignments in the Stream:

1. Click more actions button (…) to- a. Move the assignment to the top of the stream: This is a quick method to refresh the request for your stream. b. Alter the assignment c. Erase the

assignment.
2. View the number of students that have the assignment and how many haven't.
3. Click the document name to see your unique file, template, and some other resources or links you may have added with the assignment.
4. View remarks made on every individual assignment.
5. Click the assignment name to access the assignment details page.

MANAGING ASSIGNMENTS: ASSIGNMENT DETAILS

Managing Assignments on the Assignment Details Page:

Click the title of any assignment in the stream to access the assignment details page.

Every assignment has a details page where you can see which students have "submitted," or "marked as done," their assignments, evaluation and return assignments to students, and download a CSV of your evaluations/grades.

Here you can see a list of students that are either done or not with the assignment. (Use the dropdown box to swap between all, not done, and done.) You can also tap on the archive to see and evaluate their work.

MANAGING ASSIGNMENTS: ASSIGNMENT DETAILS

Instructions Tab:

There are two tabs at the top of this page. The Instructions tab will give you an overview of the assignment details and any remarks. You can also use the more action button (three specks "...") to alter or delete.

Student Work Tab:

The Student Work tab will allow you access and give direct links to every student's assignment documents if there are any available. You can without much effort click on the document link to open the student record to audit and evaluate. You can also post reviews on this page.

Grading Assignments

Grading or Evaluating Assignments on the Assignment Details Page: On the left side of the page is the place you can give grades for the assignment and return work to students.

1. Type the specific points/grades for the student.
2. Use the dropdown to choose from present grades or "ungraded."
3. Check the box alongside the student(s) names you wish to return.
4. Click on the return button to return the assignment and also notify the student.
5. Click on the email symbol to email the student.

Download a CSV of Your Grades:

If you want to download a spreadsheet of all of your evaluations/grades for your records or to bring into your grade book framework, you can download a CSV spreadsheet for every assignment or all of your assignments from the Assignment details page.

To download a CSV spreadsheet of your grades, click the settings icon close to the upper right, and select the download of your choice.

AUDITING ALL ASSIGNMENTS

Auditing Assignments on the All Assignments Page: You can also check and review assignments for ALL of your classes by going to the Assignments page. Go to the menu in the upper left (three lines), and pick Assignments.

Here you will have the accompanying choices:

- To Review: This tab will show all of the assignments that have been "turned in" for you to audit, review as well as grade.
- Reviewed: This tab will show a list of all of the assignments that you have just assessed.
- Assignment Class and Title: You can tap on the assignment name to go to the assignment details page.
- Done: See the number of students who have finished with the assignment.
- Not Done: See the number of students who are not finished with the assignment.
- Mark as Reviewed: Use this more action menu (three dots "…") to mark assignments as reviewed.

Note: There is no confirmation framework inside Google Classroom to confirm a student has finished their assignment. "Turn in" and "Mark as Done," are simply markers that the student has clicked those buttons. The teacher will, in any case, need to check for completion.

STUDENT'S VIEW: ALL ASSIGNMENTS

Student's View of Assignments Page:

Students can also observe a list of their assignments for ALL of their classes by going to the Assignments page. Go to the menu (three lines) in the upper left, and select Assignments.

There are two tabs at the top of this page:

- To-Do: Here, students can see a list of all of the assignments that are pending, including the class name, title, and due date. Click the assignment name to go to the assignment details page.
- Done: Here, students can see a list of all of the assignments they have submitted or have been marked as done.

COMMUNICATION

Class Comments vs Private Comments

Student Comment Actions:

There are two kinds of comments: class comments and private comments, which are visible to the whole class (if this has been enabled in your settings). These are marked in the comment space, yet students need to focus. Make certain to give clear guidance on where they should comment.

Student Comment Actions:

On every student post, you will have an additional action button (three dots "..."). Using this button, you can decide to:

1. Move the post to the top of the stream,
2. Delete the post,
3. Or on the other hand, bar the student. (This is helpful if a student is abusing the comments option.)

Communicating Due Dates:

Google Classroom makes it simple for students to see what assignments they have left to finish, and what is coming due soon. On the left side of the stream, students can see what assignments are due next. The mobile apps also show pop-up messages about assignments, due dates, and much more.

Automated Actions:

Google Classroom will automatically send students email notices each time you post an announcement, assignment, or questions in the class. (Note: Email notifications will only work if the email is turned on for your students through your Google App space. Students additionally can turn off email notification in their settings.)

Email Students from Google Classroom:

You can email groups of students from the Students tab inside Google Classroom. (Note: Email notices will only work if the email is turned on for your students through your Google App.)

1. Select the students or students that you might want to email using the checkbox. (Use the top checkbox to choose all students.)
2. At that point, click the Actions button and choose email.
3. Another window will pop up where you can write and send your email.

Chapter 3:

HOW TO SET UP GOOGLE CLASSROOM

So, your children are at home free from any potential harm. Now you can at least sit back and relax knowing they're in the safety of their own home, not going to class with its issues. Like what on earth is Google Classroom? How would I use it? Why are classes called "Meets?". These are the questions being raised by everybody, teachers, particularly.

We realize it may be challenging, innovation always is, particularly if you've never been required to use it. So, we thought we'd make up a quick guide on the most proficient method to use Google Classrooms, thinking of it as 'the option to in-person teaching that is being embraced by everybody'. It's not hard; it's much the same as setting up a classroom just with more screens and webcams.

Check your accounts

Now it is likely that you won't have one: however, to get to Google Classroom, you'll require a Google account. So, before we go any further just sign up for the service. Try not to stress; it's truly not a major thing. Also, you'll gain access to Google Drive, Google Calendar, Gmail, and most importantly, Google Classroom!

Class is in session

When you've signed in, this is the place you'll set up your class so we should begin by clicking the large "+" in the upper right-hand corner of the screen. Select "Create Class" and put in all the data you need. Make it simple and customize with a title, which segment you'll be instructing, and perhaps a room number to give it a feeling of school.

When your class is set up, you'll require a few students to fill it. At the top of your screen, just beneath the subject name, you'll discover a "Class Code". This is what your students will require if they are to join the class. Send this out through whatever means you believe is simplest (perhaps WhatsApp group or email) and watch as they all sign in. You can also personally invite them to join the class, but it would most likely be a lot simpler if they had a Class Code. From here, it's genuinely straight forward. All of your interactions are named clearly, from planning announcements to reacting to anything your students post. This is your main hub of engagement, so you will see a lot on this screen.

A worksheet, work smart

So, you're ready to respond to questions, at least that is an issue you don't need to worry about. Something should be said about having your students accomplish some real work? Click on the Classwork tab to begin setting up assignments for your students to work on. You can even set when you need them to hand work in through Google Calendars which will send out updates just before they need to deliver. So now they will have no reason not to submit their work on schedule; they're getting notifications the night before!

Upgrading

Finally, when everything's been done and submitted, you'll have to review your student's work and hand it back to them. This is readily done through the Grades tab, where your students will have the option to see all their past assignments and marks just to ensure they're fully up to date with everything. How many of them will make use of those older assignments when studying for tests? We'll bet on that number being low because children will be children and we've all been there.

That ought to be all you have to do immediately to go through Google Classroom with your students. Without a doubt, it's not equivalent to really sitting in school, but rather it's a well built, organized framework that should make life easier in the coming days/weeks/months. Make sure you use the rest of Google's list of online items to upgrade the learning experience much more: Google

Slides is extraordinary for making introductions, Google Meet can be used to stream your exercises, and Google Forms makes reviewing tests and assignment papers simpler than ever. Educating from home doesn't need to be troublesome, you know.

Chapter 4:

Tips to Get the Most Out of Google Classroom

A significant number of the international schools that have shut because of the lockdown have opted to use Google Classroom to educate remotely. Here they give their top tips.

With numerous schools getting ready for educating during the lockdown, you may be in search of free online technology for remote learning. There are a couple of alternatives, and we will create guides for some of these.

We focus on Google Classroom, which has been used by well-known schools that have already had to close.

We asked a few teachers already using the service for their top tips.

What's the lingo?

Google Classroom - This is the place you put your lesson materials, assignments, and announcements. Files, images, links, and videos can all be uploaded here. You can also mark work and have control over whether students have the authorization to post or comment.

Google Classroom Stream - Just like a chatroom, Google Stream permits students to ask questions and post comments.

Google Docs - somewhat like an online word archive, google docs permits you to make a document to be shared with other people.

Google Hangout - An online talk office where you can talk with or without video over the internet.

Where do I discover everything?

Fortunately, there are a lot of postings online to help you in setting up Google Classroom.

You can use the information in this book to take you through the steps of setting up your classroom.

Google Classroom is well known among teachers throughout the nation, and it's continually being refreshed. That is the reason we had to share a current analysis of the valuable ways you can use the platform with your students.

Thus, regardless of whether you're currently using Classroom or simply considering using it, read through the listings below and consider how these ideas could work for you. Want to stay up to date on new feature updates and release? Try this convenient resource to follow what's going on in the Classroom monthly

Team up with other teachers on your campus: There are lots of little tips you will learn this way. Make certain to share and work together with different teachers on your campus, so your students get a consistent message. Start a Google Doc to share your layouts.

Show Student the "Turn In" Button

When you assign a Google Slide, Doc, or Sheet as an assignment where every student gets a duplicate, you should tell students the best way to go to the record that you, the teacher, have just made and shared with them. Ensure they understand you already have the option to see their work. Show them the turn in button that comes up to one side of the blue offer button close to the top-right of the screen. A few students will be inclined to share with the teacher or create another document, so make certain to show them the method that you like. When they turn in their assignment, they will no longer have the option to edit.

Tell/Show Students The best way to Unsubmit an Assignment

As referenced above, when a student turns in their work, they will not, at this point, have the option to alter the document. If they have to return and make changes or add attachments, they have to unsubmit the task, or you, the teacher, should return it to the student.

Refresh

If there has been an update in Google Classroom while you have the page open, you will see an option to refresh to see the changes. Make sure you show students this element so they can see when you make updates to their assignments during class.

Turn in Videos or Photos of Work

Sometimes assignments are not computerized, and that is alright! You can, in any case, use Google Classroom to follow assignments and give your feedback. Have students take a picture and submit through Google Classroom. This is excellent for demonstrating the means of working through a math problem, indicating progress on results from a science lab experiment or art project. Short recordings are also an excellent choice for reflection on the learning procedure.

Submit Feedback to Google

Google Classroom is the main app developed exclusively for

education, and Google listens to your criticism! There have been enormous updates to Google Classroom throughout this year, on account of educators like you. Use the question mark at the bottom left to submit suggestions and feedbacks. They read it!

Set up all teachers with class data and registers

It's a smart idea for school leaders to set up each teacher for Google Classroom using SIMs, says Freya Odell, a teacher of English at St George's International School in Rome.

Offer planning time and training

"When we realized the schools would close, we had a training on using Google Classroom," says Odell.

All teachers got a day of CPD on the various projects, and afterward, further help was provided for any teachers who required extra assistance with setting up their classes.

The next day, exercises started.

"This gave everybody a breathing space, and meant we weren't all worried about preparing exercises straight away," she says.

Check your servers

Anything you're running from your school servers may require a bigger capacity than normal - ensure you've checked with your I.T. group that what you are planning won't overload the framework.

Don't over-muddle it

Jennie Devine, head at St Louis International school Milan, which has been shut for more than three weeks, proposes less is more when teaching remotely.

"On our initial few days, we attempted to set up videos, worksheets, quizzes, and so on - students thought that it was difficult to navigate and they didn't know what order to get things done in," she remarks. "We currently attempt to focus on an exercise video (perhaps two sections) and some other quizzes or materials appended to the exercises."

Make a daily schedule

Odell and Devine concur you have to have a framework and stick to it.

Odell recommends sorting out one folder for each day per class.

She starts every exercise with a Google Hangout in the classroom region, and afterward, students can pose questions on the Classroom Stream.

Students can finish their work and post it in the classroom.

"We can without much difficulty track who has and hasn't finished their work along these lines," says Odell.

Devine concludes that reasonable guidelines help to prevent repeated questions clogging up your notifications.

"You have to set up specific standards and practices. Comments ought to be regarding the work only, and they additionally need to look at the past comments before inquiring," she says.

Take control with your settings

In case you're not careful, the notifications can squash you - sort out your settings, so you're not being overloaded with notifications each time somebody comments on a document.

You also need to have the option to switch off when you're off - be strict with your working hours, and do not let the computer rule your life.

A lot of screen time isn't useful for your psychological wellbeing- so set "out of office" on when you have to step away from the computer.

Be realistic and clear in your instructions

Not all students will have paper materials or printers at home, says Devine, so make sure your assignments should all be possible without printing off any additional items.

"I keep the activities exceptionally clear," adds Odell. "If students feel their tech capacities are not sufficient to edit/alter the documents, at that point, they use Google Docs and simply share the link. I can post a comment directly onto their document when I feedback."

If you don't think that would work for you, another framework you should try is setting up a different assignment in the classroom for giving work in.

"I have discovered that having an everyday assignment called 'Attach work here' functions admirably for my students," says Devine. "Students can transfer all of their tasks in one go, and I can see who has finished their work.

"Otherwise, students begin appending work to video exercises, and it may be confusing if there is more than one video."

No faces in videos

All students should know to close their cameras when using Google Hangout with their teachers, says Odell. This ought to be impressed from the beginning, and all students should know to not show their faces when conversing with teachers.

Share your logins

According to security rules, I.T. staff should share teachers' logins, and no chat ought to be done on the teacher's private logins. Developers ought to be regularly checking the substance of messages.

Teachers should only speak with students using the school-endorsed channels, and students ought to be advised how to expect any communications that arrive from their teachers and to report any correspondence other than the authorized ones to the safeguarding lead.

Speak with guardians and parents

Use the classroom to keep guardians and parents on top of it. You can invite guardians and parents to follow every day or week after week with an email synopsis about what's happening in their children's classes. The messages incorporate a student's missing or upcoming work, as well as questions and messages posted by you in the class stream.

Assist students with staying organized with Google Calendar.

Classroom will produce a Google Calendar for each class and updates the calendar with students' up and coming work and due dates. Students can also see events like field trips and test dates. The calendar makes it simpler to remain on track, and since new assignments or changed due dates match up; as a result, students will always see the most up-to-date information.

Appoint work to a subset of students.

Teachers can appoint work and post announcements to students or a group of students inside a class. This usefully allows teachers to give tailored advice for differing abilities, and help with group work.

Use annotations with the versatile Classroom app.

Teachers and students can use the Classroom app on iOS, Android, and Chrome mobile phones. You can give constant feedback on student work in the app. Students can also comment on their assignments to more effectively express a concept or idea.

Explore Classroom mixes with other apparatuses.

Google Classroom uses an API to interface and share information with a large number of your preferred devices. Several apps and sites incorporate API, including Actively Learn, Pear Deck, Newsela, and many more. If you need to learn more, read chapter 10 of this book to know more about apps and sites that integrate with Google Classroom.

Encourage administrators to utilize Classroom metrics.

Although this feature is for managers - not teachers - it's of significance here. Administrators can use the Admin feature to see details, for example, what number of classes have been made, what number of posts have been sent out, and which teachers are using the tool. Access to this data can assist with personalized support for teachers.

Chapter 5:

Google Classroom Can Help With Home-Schooling

Do you take part in educating, or are you a student of any course? The free Google Classroom service can support both students and teachers. Here is how you begin.

It isn't just in school that teaching happens and education can be found in an assortment of settings.

One of the difficulties in studying is communication. This is regularly delivered through educational platforms that the school has bought. For other people, Google Classroom might be an interesting free solution.

The service was initially attached to the educational system; however, since 2017, it is available to everybody. The main requirement is that everybody who uses it has a free Google account - and, obviously, a computer or Chromebook on which to access it.

All in one place

The design of Google Classroom is straightforward. As a teacher, you can create a page for each group or class and afterward invite students. Through Google Classroom, you would then be able to send messages to all or chosen students, and it is additionally possible to schedule these communications.

The most significant function is creating learning materials. You can do this with the assistance of online tools, for example, Documents, Spreadsheets, and Presentations, Google's alternative to Microsoft Office. The class additionally has a shared folder on Google Drive, so you can share a wide range of records.

To ensure that students have learned something, you can produce schoolwork and questions. Maybe a test will make learning more fun.

Since everything is assembled in the Google Classroom, as a teacher, you can follow what a student is doing, making it very easy to give feedback.

HOW GOOGLE CLASSROOM FUNCTIONS

1. Menu

    To-do lists, calendar, class lists, and more are collected here.

2. Stream

   Here the present flow is shown.

3. Classwork

   Questions, Create materials, and assignments for the class.

4. People

   All data about the students are gathered here - and you can remove a student from the course.

5. Grades

   Google Classroom can help you grade and mark assignments.

6. Settings

   Change settings, and discover alternative routes to other Google services.

7. Class code

This code permits students to become members of the course.

8. Theme

   You can alter the theme pictured here.

9. Future tasks

   Here is the material that is coming in from the students.

10. Posts

    Share assignments, files, and links with the class.

11. Messages

    Send messages to the class; everybody can comment.

CHAPTER 6:

LOCKDOWN DRIVES IMMENSE DEMAND FOR GOOGLE CLASSROOM APP

The Google Classroom platform is a service that offers web-based learning tools through the web and an app and has been in high demand since March as schools and colleges have shut down.

The service, which was launched in 2014 followed by the app in 2015, consolidates Google Drive, Google Sheets, Google Docs, and Slides alongside Google Calendar and Gmail to permit teachers to give exercises to students. The service incorporates support for assignments and comparable coursework as well as the ability to review and grade assignments.

The Google Classroom app has consistently had clients, however, until this month had never been in the best 100 apps previously. As indicated by app tracking App Annie, the app has now hit 50 million downloads and was in the top 5 apps in the U.S a week ago. The app is also popular around the world, with an enormous spike in downloads in nations, for example, Indonesia, Finland, Italy, Mexico,

Canada, and Poland.

Students are not great fans of the service. The Telegraph announced that schoolchildren are posting on the app one-star audits in the expectation it will get brought down, and they will no longer need to go to classes remotely. Reviews for both the Android and iOS versions of the app are said to have included pleas to "let us make the most of the break."

Workplace collaboration apps are additionally surging—Microsoft Corp's. Team app added twelve million new clients in seven days against 7,000 new clients previously, while rival Slack Inc. has additionally seen expanding levels of interest and demand.

Online association apparatuses now rule app records, with Zoom Video Communications Inc's. Video conferencing app topping the free app download market. Other well-known correspondence apps in the top 10 incorporate WhatsApp in 6th spot, Hangouts Meet in 7th, Facebook Inc's. Messenger in 8th and Microsoft Teams in the 9th.

HOW TO USE GOOGLE CLASSROOM WHEN YOU'RE HOMESCHOOLING DURING THE LOCKDOWN

WITH schools across the nation shut temporarily, the task of homeschooling your children can be an overwhelming one.

However, it doesn't need to be.

Google Classroom is intended to improve the home learning experience for both the children and parents.

What is Google classroom?

Classroom saves paper and time and makes it simple to create classes, communicate, distribute assignments, and remain organized.

You create assignments and projects within the app and then be able to share them with your students through email with deadlines.

Google Classroom uses Google Docs, meaning that you can go paperless with your learning.

How do I use Google Classroom?

The app is free and can be downloaded from the Google Play app store.

It can be used on a smartphone, laptop, or tablet.

Create dedicated folders for every one of your youngster's subjects, and you can upload tasks and worksheets to every one of these folders for your children to finish.

By using the Google calendar, you can set deadlines for each assignment, implying that both you and your kids can monitor what is being finished.

This means you can monitor what work has been finished – and chase up any late projects.

If you need to check your child's knowledge, you can create your tests on the Google Forum.

How to set up Google Classroom?

Start by visiting the site classroom.google.com.

There you can set up a free account using your email address.

Create classes by tapping the "+" button in the upper right-hand corner and choosing "make a class." Fill in the subtitles as indicated by the subject.

You can add assignments to each "class" by clicking on updates and afterward the "+" button.

Include exercise material using your Google Drive - this could be a YouTube video or a worksheet.

You would then be able to invite your students to your class by getting them to sign in to the classroom with the unique code you have sent to them.

Google Classroom makes a Drive folder for each new class you make - the folders show up as "class tiles".

All of your assignments and exercise material will be saved to each tile with any work your children complete being saved there as well.

Is Google Classroom any good?

Guardians who have used the app have commended its structure with regards to home learning.

Evaluating the app, one mum said: "If you don't have Google Classroom, you truly need it. It helps you to keep up with all your work.

Concurring, a second stated: "Allows my little girl to interact with school and allows her to catch up with missing work."

CHAPTER 7:

EFFECTIVENESS OF GOOGLE CLASSROOM

Teachers' perceptions:

Innovation has gained in significance in all phases of education. Yet, educators have been unable to make sense of which of the many available technological devices best fit their classroom practices. Google Classroom is one such app that is free from cost and has gained acceptance very quickly.

The primary purpose of the study is to survey teachers' recognition of the adequacy of Google Classroom. The study is carried out through a subjective research plan. The sample of the study, which uses a semi-organized meeting technique, comprised of 12 advanced education teachers who have used Google Classroom for at least one semester in their classroom.

The information obtained has been gained through an in-depth examination by coding and sorting the information through NVivo. This showed that teachers see it as just a help apparatus that can be used for record management and essential classroom management, without significantly affecting education strategies. The reactions of the teachers show that the absence of easy to understand interface is the primary purpose behind its inefficiency.

Problem Statement

With the target of expanding classroom usability, teachers mean to improve student commitment by making student experience increasingly personalized and independent, an expanding number of schools, universities, and advanced education institutes are in the process of adopting mixed learning (Spring, Hadlock, and Graham, 2016). Google Classroom can be useed as a blended learning instrument to reduce classroom costs. The lack of research on Google classroom, particularly with regards to developing nations, has increased the need to further explore the viability of the device. Properly using technology is probably the greatest test for the teachers to manage in a blended learning condition; this study is centered around evaluating the adequacy of Google Classroom in advanced education classes.

Teaching Listening Skill through Google Classroom

Among the four language skills, ESL students consider listening skills to be the most difficult one to learn. In Bangladesh, both students and teachers give excuses to stay away from this significant language skill at intermediate, elementary, and tertiary levels. Teachers worldwide are moving towards e-learning in ELT, and Google Classroom is one of them. This blended learning stage offers various benefits of Google to improve the teaching-learning process for both the students and teachers. These days students at the tertiary level are open to innovations. This book exhibits how a language teacher can encourage the technophile ESL students to build up their listening expertise in Google Classroom and the effects it has on students.

Chapter 8:

Benefits and Limitations of Google Classroom

This platform has various useful elements. Some of them are referenced below:

- User friendly: It is quite easy to use. As M. Janzen brings up, "Google Classroom's plan intentionally simplifies the instructional interface and alternatives used for delivering and tracking assignments; correspondence with the whole course or individuals is also improved through email, messages, and push notifications".
- Cloud-based: Google Classroom offers increasingly proficient and useable innovation to use in the learning environment as Google apps represent a significant element of cloud-based communications used all through the professional workforce.
- Cost-free: It doesn't require any expense to use it. Anybody with or without an institutional Google account can create and join a classroom.
- Cell phone friendly: As M. Janzen states, "Mobile access to learning materials that are appealing and simple to cooperate with is basic in the present web associated learning

environments". Google Classroom is easy to use on any mobile phone.
- Time-saving: Google Classroom saves time both for students and teachers alike. As indicated by Iftakhar, "It synchronizes other Google apps like Slides, Docs, Drive, and Spreadsheets. However, the entire procedure of administering grading, assignments, reviewing, formative evaluation, and feedback is uncomplicated and streamlined".

LIMITATIONS

Despite the numerous advantages, there are a few restrictions on Google Classroom. The followings are some of them as referenced by C. Pappas:

- Limited integration options: Google Classroom isn't synchronized with Google Calendar or some other calendar. It gets hard for the teacher to sort out teaching materials and set cut off times for assignments.
- Too "googlish": Pappas characterizes Google Classroom as a lot of "googlish". It is equipped with a few buttons which are well-known to Google clients. Because of this, the individuals who are the first time users (students at primary and secondary levels for instance) of Google items may get confused or take more time to get acquainted with the symbols. Only YouTube

is coordinated with Google Classroom to help video sharing. Other well-known tools like SlideShare, Facebook, and so forth are not worked in with Google Classroom.

- No mechanized updates: Google Classroom doesn't make the update on activity-feeds automatically. Students need to refresh for updates; they may miss a significant announcement.
- Difficult student sharing: Sharing a file with different classmates is impossible if a student doesn't turn into the owner of a file. However, if they become the owner of a file, they will require permission from the teacher to share their archive.
- Editing issues: After creating and circulating an assignment, students become owners of the archive. As the owner, they are given the authority to alter it. They can delete any piece of the assignment if they want.
- No automated tests and quizzes: Google Classroom has no facility for computerized tests and quizzes. Therefore, it does not completely replace other accessible Learning Management Systems (LMS). In most cases, Google Classroom is more useful as a blended learning stage than a completely online LMS.
- Impersonal: Even though it is offering a blended learning stage, it has not coordinated other chatting apps like Google Hangouts. Unfortunately, it is extremely unlikely to have a live chat in Google Classroom; at least, not yet.

GOOGLE CLASSROOM FOR TEACHING LISTENING ABILITIES

To observe the effect of Google Classroom for teaching listening aptitude, the specialists have defined the following research structure for the study and made a couple of recommendations.

The study is action research conducted among 40 college students of Daffodil International University, Bangladesh. The samples are standard first-year students of B.A. in English Program. For gathering information, scientists have adopted a quantitative research technique. Statistical examination such as relative percentages and frequencies of students-performances have been collected from four distinct assignments on listening expertise. The analysts have used help from listenaminute.com for structuring research tools.

To lead the study, a classroom titled "Listening Skill" has been made by the scientists in Google Classroom, and students have been asked to join. As the students use their Gmail accounts with a comparative domain (given by the University), it is simple for them to join the classroom. The analysts produced four assignments on listening aptitude to be submitted on four consecutive weeks. The assignments are basic exercises on gap-filling while at the same time listening in.

It has been observed by ELT specialists that "Listening Skill" is one of the most difficult ones among the four language skills.

Bangladeshi students are falling behind in improving their listening expertise in English. In any case, the younger population is techno-skilled which is a benefit for the ELT experts doing research. Thinking about it as a benefit, this shows how Google Classroom can be used as a learning apparatus to upgrade students' listening skills.

Consequently, the positive effects of using Google Classroom for the students at the tertiary level shows its value.

Chapter 9:

Awesome Apps That Incorporate With Google Classroom

Many education apps work with Google Classroom. These integrations spare teachers and students time and make it simpler to share data between the Classroom and their favorite apps.

Use this listing to investigate apps you are currently using, or find new ones that will permit you to share effectively with Google Classroom.

Did you understand that Google Classroom integrates well with others?

It's hard to believe, but it's true! Google is known for making their apps open to working with outside apps, and Google Classroom is no different.

I have assembled a list of several Apps that Incorporate with Google Classroom, making it much simpler to create messages and lessons with your favorite resources and apps.

HOW TO USE THESE APPS WITH GOOGLE CLASSROOM

The vast majority of the apps below function with Google Classroom through a "share button." This association permits you to use a portion of your preferred sites and apps routinely with Google Classroom. Note: some of these apps are free, but not all.

To use the app with Google Classroom,

1. Create an account on the website or app
2. Create or locate the resources or activity within a website or app
3. Use the "Share to Classroom" option within the chosen app. (The first time you use the association you should allow authorizations to access your account.)
4. This association or connection will permit you to do things like making a test and send it to one of your classes in Google Classroom.

Actively Learn

Actively Learn works flawlessly with Google Classroom. Teachers can without much difficulty synchronize Classroom programs to

Actively Learn and adjust Actively Learn grades and assignments back to Google Classroom.

Additio App

Additio App is a suite for teachers to remain in control and easily contact students and families. It offers numerous helpful tools, similar to an amazing grade-book and a strong exercise organizer.

Aeries

Teachers can connect to or make new Classroom classes dependent on their Aeries classes, and import scores into the Aeries grade book.

Aladdin

With this connected to Classroom, classes can be integrated with classes in Aladdin. Grades and assignments can also be matched up among Aladdin and Classroom.

Alma

Alma is the principal Student Information System to incorporate directly with Google Classroom. With this connected, teachers can synchronize grades and assignments, and tech groups can manage Google Classroom classes over their schools and locale.

American Museum of Natural History

Educational K-12 projects and resources from the American Museum of Natural History. Use the Share to Classroom button to share applicable articles, resources, and curriculum.

Aristotle Insight: K12

Enable students to become insightful, with this all-in-one borderless classroom management.

ASSISTments

Offers feedback to teachers and students synchronously when students complete assignments using this free online device.

BookWidgets

BookWidgets gives layouts for interactive activities. Teachers can pick between more than 40 distinct gadgets or layouts to connect with students.

BrainPOP

With BrainPOP, teachers can import their classes legitimately from Google Classroom into My BrainPOP. SSO-prepared student accounts are made when a teacher imports a class, permitting students to sign in to BrainPOP through the Google launcher menu.

Buncee

A creation and introduction apparatus for students and teachers to make interactive classroom content, permitting students of any age to visualize concepts and communicate creatively Just build a task, note, class update, action, or undertaking, and share it with the students in your Google Classroom.

CK-12

CK-12 Foundation gives a library of free online videos, textbooks, flashcards, exercises, and genuine apps for more than 5000 ideas from arithmetic to history.

Classcraft

With the Classcraft integration, teachers can pull lists from Google

Classroom and accounts in a single click. Teachers can give students points in the game for turning in assignments on schedule and convert their Classroom results into game points.

CodeHS

CodeHS is a far-reaching platform for helping schools teach software engineering. They give online educational plans, teaching aids and resources, and professional advancement.

Curiosity.com Their point of interest is to ignite curiosity and inspire individuals to learn. Every day, they make and publish engaging topics for many interested students around the world.

Desmos

An assortment of remarkable and engaging digital math activities, which are free for you and your students.

Discovery Education

Discovery Education ignites student interest and moves instructors to rethink learning with award-winning advanced content and professional improvement.

Dogo News

DOGO Media is the main online network enabling children to see news using online media in a fun, protected, and social environment. used by a large number of students and teachers from around the globe, their sites have immediately become a network of children and instructors connecting with recent developments, books, and films.

DuoLingo

Numerous teachers and even entire governments around the globe now see Duolingo as the ideal blended learning ally for their language classrooms. Duolingo exercises give every student personalized practice and feedback, enabling them to take advantage of classroom guidance.

Edcite

Teachers can import their class programs from Google Classroom into Edcite, and afterward, send Edcite assignments to their students in the classroom. At the point when students get to these assignments, they are automatically signed into their Edcite accounts using single sign-on.

EdPuzzle

Create an interactive video lesson, include your magical touch, and track your student's understanding. With the EDpuzzle integration, teachers can import all Classroom courses and students at sign up.

Edulastic

Synchronizing with Google Classroom makes class lists in Edulastic and stays up to date. Teachers would then be able to share Edulastic appraisals directly in student's classroom feeds, permitting them to get to the task without entering another password or going to the Edulastic site.

Engage NY

With EngageNY in the classroom, students get immediate feedback on their work, with repeat attempts if necessary, while teachers can without much difficulty access information to drive their in-class instruction.

Explain Everything

Thanks to this Google Classroom incorporation, teachers and administrators can flawlessly oversee licenses using Explain Everything Discover.

Flat

Teachers can make music composition and structure assignments in Google Classroom using Flat Education, online music documentation programming. Teachers can synchronize existing Classroom lists and structure new music exercises open to students from the classroom.

Flipgrid

Flipgrid is a site that permits teachers to make "frameworks" of short conversation style questions that students react to through recorded videos. Every framework is a message board where teachers can pose questions, and their students can post 90-second video reactions that show up in a tiled "grid" show. Effectively share links to Flipgrids and add them to assignments in Google Classroom.

Familiarity Tutor for Google

Familiarity Tutor is an online app that has tools to allow students to work on reading out loud and to record sections called "appraisals" or tests. Effectively you can assign reading sections as assignments in Google Classroom.

Gale Cengage Learning

Gale examination resources incorporate novel online databases, essential library sources, advanced paper files, courses, eBooks, and print books.

GAT+

Monitor student's conduct on Chrome devices and G Suites with this audit and security apparatus.

GeoGebra

GeoGebra's K-12+ STEM educational program materials can be embedded into Google Classroom as activities with only a couple of clicks. More than 700,000 materials (in addition to more included every day!) are accessible to meet the STEM needs of teachers and students.

GoGuardian

GoGuardian Teacher permits teachers to indicate the classrooms they've set up in the Classroom, adjusting student enlistment, class period, and subject across platforms. Teachers and students can profit considerably more from their Chromebooks with streamlined usage and setup.

Google Cast for Education

Google Cast for Education is a free Chrome app that permits students and teachers to share their screens remotely from anyplace in the classroom. The cast for education has built-in controls for teachers and permits them to easily add students from the classroom.

InsertLearning

InsertLearning is a Chrome augmentation that lets you transform sites into intelligent exercises. You can include notes, videos, discussion questions, links, multiple-choice questions, and more! Then effectively share your exercise with students in Google Classroom.

Kami

With the Kami app, teachers can transform assignments, worksheets, and educational program resources in PDF format for students to finish and then submit.

Khan Academy

Khan Academy supports teachers with thoroughly customized learning devices and information-driven bits of knowledge – all for free. Teachers can import their Google Classroom programs into Khan Academy and directly assign Khan Academy content to their students through the classroom.

Kodable

Kodable instructs children to code at home or school with fun games and gives teachers a total K-5 coding educational plan for the classroom.

LearnZillion

LearnZillion is a site that furnishes teachers with a library of intelligent math and language art exercises, quizzes, videos, and assignments for students. LearnZillion tracks student progress and achievement on the exercises and tests and reports the outcomes to the teacher's dashboard for assessment.

Little SIS for Classroom

Little SIS for Classroom creates Google Classroom classes and auto-synchronizes class lists from student data, making it simpler for schools to embrace and keep up Google Classroom.

Listenwise

Listenwise is an award-winning listening ability platform. They harness the intensity of tuning in to propel education and learning in all students. Their assortment of digital recordings and open radio continues instructing associated with current reality and builds student listening aptitudes simultaneously.

LucidPress

Lucidpress is an online-based drag and drop publishing app, enabling anybody to make stunning material for digital and print.

Makers Empire 3D

Makers Empire 3D is intended to help K-8 teachers coordinate 3D plans and printing into their teaching practice efficiently and effectively.

Math Games

This integration aligns Classroom with MathGames.com, a hotspot for math games, and aptitude practice on the web. Teachers can automatically create and match up math assignments within the classroom and keep tabs on student's development.

Nearpod

Nearpod is a student engagement platform that can be used to amazing effect in the classroom. The app's idea is basic. A teacher can make presentations that can contain Quiz's, Videos, Polls, Images, Web Content, Drawing-Boards, etc.

NetTrekker

Permits teachers and students to look through 360,000+ educator-vetted guidelines, adjusted, open education resources all in one place.

Newsela

With the Google Classroom integration, teachers using Newsela can sign up, import classrooms, and share assignments with Google Classroom. This makes it quicker and simpler for teachers to begin using Newsela.

OpenEd.com

Teachers can assign OpenEd assessments, games, videos, and repeat questions with a single click, and finished assignments will be stamped "done". OpenEd additionally gives group and single sign-on, so all classes and students will be matched up routinely.

Chapter 10:

Frequently Asked Questions

What is Google Classroom?

Google depicts Google Classroom as "mission control for your classroom," and this may be the simplest way to consider it. It's a platform that integrates Google's G Suite programs for students and teachers. It additionally acts as a computerized coordinator where teachers can prepare class materials and share them with students - all paperlessly. This adaptability, and its integration with Google's famous tools, is probably what's made Google Classroom one of the most broadly used EdTech systems today.

Is Google Classroom an LMS?

In fact, no. Google Classroom isn't a course management system (CMS), learning management system (LMS), or student information system (SIS). So, Google routinely adds new functions to Google Classroom. In June 2019, for instance, Google reported that schools would before long have the option to adjust the systems' new evaluating highlights to a current student data framework. As Google keeps on including updates, it will begin to look and work more like an LMS. However, for the time being, it's ideal to think about the device as a one-stop-shop for the class organization.

How Do I Create A Class?

Is registration needed?

To use Google Classroom, just a Google account login (Gmail address) is needed. If you need to create another one, head to accounts.google.com, click Create Account, choose For Myself, at that point, fill in the necessary data.

Now log on to classroom.google.com, click Open Classroom, and sign in.

Who Can Use Google Classroom?

Anybody! Google Classroom is available as a free service for anybody with a Google account, and it's free for organizations using G Suite for Education or G Suite for Nonprofits. Generally, students and teachers can get to Google Classroom using a Google account given by their school. While students and teachers in schools are the main clients of Google Classroom, there are also features that families, and home-schoolers, and administrators can use.

How Do I Create A Class?

As a teacher, you would now need to create a class. To do this, click on the plus icon at the upper right and select Create Course. Acknowledge the terms, name the course, fill in other data, and confirm with Create. You now see the course code and course name.

How Would I Invite Students?

A student can join your course by heading to Google Classroom, tapping the + link, and afterward picking Join course as opposed to Create course. Enter the class code and select Join.

As should be obvious, the same service is used for both students and teachers - so you can take on the roles in different settings.

Would I Be Able To Use My Mobile Phone?

Google Classroom is accessible as an app, for both and iPhone/iPad and Android. To download it, look for Google Classroom on the App Store or Google Play Store.

Is It Open To All Teachers?

If you are a teacher at a school, you can't use the free version of Google Classroom. Rather, the school must secure G Suite for Education, and it is a choice that the school management must make. Among the reasons behind this, GDPR has clear principles on how students' personal information may be handled.

How Do Teachers Use Google Classroom?

Since it's a genuinely adaptable system, teachers can use its features in various ways. With Google Classroom, teachers can:

Streamline how they oversee classes. The program incorporates Google's different devices like Drive, Docs, and Calendar, so there are loads of inherent "alternate ways" for classroom-management of assignments. For instance, if you post an assignment with a due date, it's automatically added to the class schedule for your students to see.

Digitally compose, distribute, and gather course materials, assignments, and student work. Teachers can post an assignment to different classes or adjust and reuse assignments from year to year. If your students have normal access to devices, Google Classroom can assist you with printer use and cut down the amount of paper consumed that comes with learning and teaching.

Communicate with students about their classwork. You can use the platform to post reminders and messages about assignments, and it's easy to see who has or hasn't finished their work. You can also check in with individual students privately, answer their questions, and offer help.

Give students feedback on their assessments and assignment. Within Google Classroom, it's possible to use Google Forms to make and share tests that are reviewed as students turn them in. You'll spend less time grading, but your students will get instant feedback on their work.

How Do I Set Up My Google Classroom?

The essential setup process for Google Classroom is entirely intuitive, even for first-time clients. The Google Teacher Center offers a few instructional exercises for getting started - this is your best option if you're searching for the most up to date information and videos. There are also a lot of instructional videos on YouTube posted by tech-integration specialists and teachers. A significant number of these teacher-made recordings incorporate practical tips and tricks they've learned from using the platform in their classrooms.

What Is Google Doing With My Students' Information? Should I Be Worried About Privacy?

As a teacher, protecting your students' information and privacy should be a consideration whenever you're picking a computerized platform for your classroom. Whenever a device may gather information from students, it's critical to ask about how the organizations involved are making sure about, using, and storing student information.

Google says that information security and privacy is a high priority for all G Suite for Education items. Nonetheless, teachers should remember that guardians and families have a right to opt-out if they don't want kids using Google programs in the school. Before launching Google Classroom, school teachers and administrators should have an alternative arrangement set up for students who may decide to opt-out.

In the past, a few instructors, families, and supporters have expressed doubts about Google's capacity to deliver on promises about security and information privacy. Also, the noticeable quality of Google products and branding in schools has brought up issues about the trade-offs of permitting Google to show its brand in schools. Whether you use Google Classroom or not, it's essential to get students thinking critically about information security and the commercialization we see in various parts of our lives - including our classrooms.

How can parents and families stay in the loop with Google Classroom?

Google Classroom has choices for teachers to send reminders about students' classwork; however, it doesn't offer the degree of correspondence you'll discover in devices like ClassDojo, SeeSaw, or Remind. Google alludes to families and guardians as "guardians" who can get email synopses about missing work, upcoming work, and different class arrangements. It doesn't incorporate highlights for direct messaging with families or permit families to make comments on their kids' work.

What's new in Google Classroom?

The platform has been refreshed a considerable amount since its launch, and Google keeps on presenting upgrades, frequently as a result of criticism from teachers. For quite a while, clients have been criticizing Google Classroom's lack of reviewing highlights or a tool for making headings. Google listened and is revealing these new highlights for the 2019-2020 school year. Note that for the time being, to get the new headings and grade-matching up features, administrators or teachers should sign up for a pilot program.

How can I make Google Classroom more interactive and engaging for my students?

To make learning with advanced projects progressively effective for students, consider mixing up the sorts of resources you share with them in Google Classroom. Even though G Suite has devices like Google Slides and Google Docs, students and teachers can share different sorts of media, including pictures, YouTube videos, screencasts, and links to websites. A few teachers even give students an assortment of choices for presenting their work within Google Classroom. For instance, you may offer students the option to respond to reading assignments with a video clip, comment, or drawings that show their reasoning.

In case you're looking to create an intelligent center point for students, you might consider doing this on Google Classroom's Stream page. Within Google Classroom, the stream is where everybody in the class can discover future assignments and announcements, and it's the main thing students see when they sign in. Alice Keeler, a notable blogger who comments widely on Google Classroom, advises using the stream to post your class plan and suggests using Screencastify to post video messages for students.

A few teachers go through the stream to set class conversation sheets, where students can associate online by posing questions or commenting on one another's posts. These conversation sheets can help increase class interest and offer students greater value in having their voices heard by the class. With conversations, you can use the stream as a closed social network of sorts, and it could be a great method to assist kids with working on using a wide range of various citizenship skills in a "walled garden" kind of setting.

Where would I find more ideas about using Google Classroom?

In case you're searching for authentic data about Google Classroom, look at Google for Education's Twitter channel for ideas, thoughts for teachers, recordings, and even a pamphlet about G Suite for Education items. Many Google Classroom fans are also blogging, tweeting, and podcasting the many different ways of using the system with students. With a large number of teachers and ed-tech experts field-testing, testing, and advancing with Google Classroom, it's not hard to track down tips and inspiration from fellow educators on the web.

As you're using Google Classroom, don't be reluctant to get inventive with your techniques, and imaginative uses for the platform. Like most tech instruments, Google Classroom is what you make of it, and how it works will appear to be different from classroom to classroom. What's most significant is to find the methodologies and instruments inside Google Classroom that work best for you and your students. You can share the methods in which you're using Google Classroom with your students by leaving a Teacher Review.

CONCLUSION

Google Classroom is probably best described as a great start. It's intuitive, with lots of truly useful features for teachers and students, which could potentially help cut down on paper used in classrooms. But replacing a full-featured learning management system with it is not necessarily a good idea, either. It has no automated quizzes or exams, it can't connect students automatically, and it embraces far more of a blended learning model than a completely/asynchronous online one.

Google Classroom has not had a major effect on classroom teaching. It has been used adequately for transferring assignments, classroom management, and communication with the students; nonetheless, the general use is restricted to these features. An attractive point is that it is a free device and has no cost implications. These are early days for Google Classroom, and recognize that this platform will develop over time. A significant finding of the study was that the integration of Google Classroom isn't seen as easy to understand by the teachers. If the developers can improve usability and making it easier with some extra features, for example, video streaming, then the effectiveness of Google Classroom can improve radically

Where can I find more ideas about using Google Classroom?

In case you're searching for genuine information about Google Classroom, look at Google for Education's Twitter channel for reviews, ideas for teachers, videos, and even a bulletin about G Suite for Education items. Many Google Classroom fans are also tweeting, blogging, and even, podcasting about how they're using the platform with students. With a huge number of teachers and education tech specialists field-testing and improving with Google Classroom, it's easy to find tips and inspiration from individual teachers on the web.

As you're using Google Classroom, don't be afraid to get creative with your methods, and creative uses of the platform. Like most tech tools, Google Classroom is what you make of it, and how it works will probably appear to be different from classroom to classroom. What's most important is to discover the methods and tools inside Google Classroom that works best for you and your students. You can share how you're using Google Classroom with your students by leaving a Teacher Review.

The concept of education has experienced a significant shift, lately, from teacher-driven to student or learning-driven. In the past, teachers assumed the role of information suppliers, but now their job has expanded. There is a great deal of emphasis on integrating technology/innovation in the classroom through inventive teaching methodologies that emphasize empowering students to accomplish the ideal learning goals (Hwang, Wang, and Lai, 2015).

Promoters of using educational technologies have discovered a center ground through hybrid learning (Hinkelman, 2018). The terms hybrid learning, mixed-mode learning, and blended learning are used (Breslow and Zhao, 2013). Blended learning permits smooth progress from a shift in teaching strategy for students and teachers. Significantly, the objective shouldn't be simply to incorporate technology in the classroom; rather, educational targets should determine the diverse method of teaching methods (Kristine and O'Byrne, 2015).

Teachers can now use various educational technologies, alongside the conventional classroom arrangement, to improve the learning experience for the students. In 2014, Google Application for Education (GAFE) launched Google Classroom. The app can be used by both students and teachers, which makes it a perfect fit for developing nations, where the budgets are constrained. It can be introduced as a learning management framework in schools, universities, and advanced education institutes. Teachers can make better use of classroom time by adopting Google Classroom.

www.ingramcontent.com/pod-product-compliance
Lightning Source LLC
Chambersburg PA
CBHW051540240526
45465CB00028B/1559